CONTE

CW00364056

Karl Pendlebury	31
Rehenara Begum	32
Danielle Smethurst	33
Chelsea Smith	34
Robert May	35
Abdul Wahid	36
Erin McIntyre	37
Lauren Baxendale	38
Danielle Keegan	39
Hazel Hill	40
Nathan Gammack	41
Craig Booth	42
Syed Uddin	43
Stuart Parkinson	44
Aidan Potter	45
Rehana Khan	46
Chelsea Scholes	47
Daniel Gammack	48

St Andrew's CE Primary School

Jonathan Lang	49
Hannah Howarth	50
Samuel Tonkinson	51
Mark Calland	52
Sophie Baker	53
Ian Wilkinson	54
Thomas Gidman	55
Lauren Ainscough	56
Daniel Bailey	57
Matthew Storosh	58
Nicki Russell	59
Benjamin Peter Healey	60
Reham Jusub	61
Suraiya Patel	62
Kieran M J Peat	63
Jennifer Hails	64
Andrew C Gregory	65
Christopher Jones	66

POETIC VOYAGES BOLTON

Edited by Dave Thomas

First published in Great Britain in 2001 by
YOUNG WRITERS
Remus House,
Coltsfoot Drive,
Peterborough, PE2 9JX
Telephone (01733) 890066

HB ISBN 0 75433 158 X
SB ISBN 0 75433 159 8

FOREWORD

Young Writers was established in 1991 with the aim to promote creative writing in children, to make reading and writing poetry fun.

This year once again, proved to be a tremendous success with over 88,000 entries received nationwide.

The Poetic Voyages competition has shown us the high standard of work and effort that children are capable of today. It is a reflection of the teaching skills in schools, the enthusiasm and creativity they have injected into their pupils shines clearly within this anthology.

The task of selecting poems was therefore a difficult one but nevertheless, an enjoyable experience. We hope you are as pleased with the final selection in *Poetic Voyages Bolton* as we are.

Sonia Girling	101
Jason Cullen	102
Lauren Ratcliffe	103
Callum Smith	104
Charlotte Deegan	105
Craig White	106
Rebecca Kearney	107
Jason Harrison	108
Keith Raraty	109
Alyce Garrett	110
Sally Fletcher	111
George Smyth	112
Michala Smith	113

St Stephen's CE Primary

John Knowles	114
Daniel Barlow	115
Michael Pollitt	116
Jessica Dempsey	117
Lauren Cox	118
Christina Bridge	119
Lindsey Arlington	120
Zak Stuart	121
Timothy Berry	122
Caitlin Parr	123
Luke Haslam	124
Lydia Baldwin	125
Rochelle Richards	126
Abigail Thomas	127
Leah Shayler	128

St Thomas Of Canterbury RC Primary School

Gabrielle Hamer	129
Michael Meator	130
Christina Gordon	131
Sam Horrocks	132
Andrew McCrae	133
Etienne Littlefair	134

The Poems

THE REINDEER

Once I saw a reindeer,
Soaring through the sky,
It looked very funny,
As it didn't have wings to fly.

This reindeer had massive antlers,
And a big, red, shiny nose,
And the country that it came from,
Nobody probably knows.

Rupert Grimshaw (10)
Horwich Parish CE Primary School

PEACE

Peace is white,
It smells like a beautiful flower,
Peace tastes sweet like sugar,
It sounds silent,
It feels like a cool breeze on a spring morning,
Peace lives where there are good people.

Robert Fitton (10)
Horwich Parish CE Primary School

YOUNG

Young is yellow
and smells brand new,
tastes fresh
and feels like newly baked bread,
and it lives in our world.

Charlotte Deighton (9)
Horwich Parish CE Primary School

Rainbow

Raining when the sun is out a beautiful rainbow appears
Orange sparkling throughout the sky
Yellow raging around the sky like a firework
Gorgeous glinting green glittering across the world
Bright blue oozing around the sky like a rocket
I stare as the world goes by
Velvet spread across the world like a sheet.

Lauren Charleston (10)
Horwich Parish CE Primary School

A MAGGOT

I'm a harmless maggot,
a meal for a fish,
I come in different colours,
a very tasty dish!

I hate being a maggot,
you don't live for long,
and when I'm just about to die,
I sing a peaceful song.

Matthew Jones (10)
Horwich Parish CE Primary School

FIRSTS

First glowing light,
First giggling laugh,
First ever clever word,
First splashy bath.

First exciting birthday,
First sparkling star,
First ever potty training,
First ride in a car.

First colourful picture,
First read of a book,
First gleaming snow,
I had to look.

First wrote a word,
First ever friend,
First long night,
Thought it wouldn't end.

Rachel Barnes (10)
Horwich Parish CE Primary School

THE COLOURFUL RAINBOW

Red, gorgeous, multicoloured splash of art
bursting across the sky.
Orange tingling, climbing silently
showing its colours away.
Yellow is a lemon oozing its juice out.
Gleaming, green, glistening in the clouds.
Baffling, blue, appearing as the world stares.
Indigo is an illusion spraying over the world.
Vanishing violet disappearing where the poem ends.

Natalie Halton (10)
Horwich Parish CE Primary School

MY PET HAMSTER

My pet hamster is
Ginger and fluffy
He plays in his plastic wheel
and his name is Buffy.

My pet hamster
Has a best friend
He lives next door
and his name is Fred.

My pet hamster
He lives in a cage
He sleeps all day
isn't that strange?

Alexandra Edge (10)
Horwich Parish CE Primary School

ANGER

It is black,
It smells of gas,
Nobody knows what it tastes of.
It sounds like roaring,
It is rough,
It lives in the garage.

Jac McVean (9)
Horwich Parish CE Primary School

CASTLE

Big stone walls
With guns on top
The flags are blowing
Gates make us stop

Through the gate
Soldiers stand
Guarding the treasure
Of this great land

Inside the building
Swords and shields
Medals of honour
From fighting in great fields

Great big dungeons
Great big halls
Stirling Castle
Is the best of all.

Matthew Mather (10)
Horwich Parish CE Primary School

PEACE

Peace is cream,
It smells like flowers in the small breeze.
Peace tastes sweet and fresh,
It sounds like birds singing.
It feels smooth,
It lives deep in your heart.

Perri Hughes (10)
Horwich Parish CE Primary School

MY BED

My bed is a slumber haven
A palace without walls
I lie there lost in pleasant lands
Until my mother calls.

My alarm clock won't stop ringing
I could stay in bed all day
But I know that isn't possible
What would my teacher say!

Elizabeth Roath (9)
Horwich Parish CE Primary School

THE DAYS OF THE WEEK

Monday is miserable, brown and gloomy.
Tuesday is terrible, red with anger.
Wednesday is wonderful, pink and joyful.
Thursday is thunder, black and grey.
Friday is frightening, deep and dark.
Saturday is sad, blue and tearful
And Sunday is sunny, orange and bright.

Gemma Hamer (9)
Horwich Parish CE Primary School

PEACE

Peace is yellow,
It smells like fresh blooming flowers,
It tastes like chocolate.
Peace sounds like laughter,
It feels like smooth, wet grass,
It lives in everyone's hearts.

Brogan Gilchrist (9)
Horwich Parish CE Primary School

HOPE

Hope is cream
Hope smells like flowers in the garden.
It tastes like water
It sounds like birds singing.
Hope feels soft and warm
Hope lives everywhere.

Holly Walmsley (10)
Horwich Parish CE Primary School

TOUGH ENOUGH

Are you tough enough to go one on one?
One on one with the Great One.
Or maybe you'd like to go for the Last Ride,
Maybe a Swanton Bomb.

Look, it's Stone Cold Steve Austin,
Austin's strutting down the ramp.
Now he's climbing in the ring
And the crowd's chanting 'Austin 3:16'.

A stunner here, a stunner there,
Wrestlers flying round the ring.
Now he's rolled out of the squared circle
And is walking up the bloodthirsty ramp.

The Dudley Boyz are walking down the ramp,
Buh Buh Ray Dudley scoop slams
Then shouts out *'Whassap'*!
And D-Von plants his head on the man's chest.

Mark Bromley (9)
Horwich Parish CE Primary School

MY PET SNAKE

My pet Gunter
is a hissy snake
his eyes are black, his tail is red
and he does a little shake.

My pet Gunter
is very hissy
and it sounds like a motor
his belly is very fizzy.

Mortiz Bromley (9)
Horwich Parish CE Primary School

HAIKUS

Winter:

> Frozen cold mornings,
> Robins fly in the cold air,
> Children are playing.

Summer:

> Flowers pop up new,
> The summer sun is shining,
> You hear the birds sing.

Autumn:

> Autumn is breezy,
> Bonfires are just beginning,
> I hear the leaves fall.

Spring:

> Spring is in the air,
> Blossoms are germinating,
> Spring is very bright.

Scott Lees (10)
Our Lady of Lourdes RC Primary School

GROWLING STORMS

You can hear the rumble in the sky
you can see the zigzag when it strikes.
You can hear the violence of the cloud
makes the thunder appear out loud.
You can hear a growl
after the howl.
In the sky you hear *crash*
on the cloud you see the *clash.*
Use your ears and hear the bangs
look at the clouds in a shape of fangs.
Look at the trees when they clash
look at the lightning as it smashes.

Kyle Clugston (10)
Our Lady of Lourdes RC Primary School

DOWN IN THE JUNGLE

Down in the jungle you might see a monkey in a banana tree.
Under the water in the mud and murk, a crocodile is sure to lurk.
He's not very fat, he's got much thinner
that's why he'll eat you up for dinner.

Stacey Daley (10)
Our Lady of Lourdes RC Primary School

LIGHTS, CAMERA, ACTION

Act one; scene one:

Cameras are rolling
Rehearsals are done
Actors are nearly on stage.

The director shouts 'Action'
The curtain goes up
What a stunning reaction
As the audience stands up.

Spotlights are blazing
In front of the packed house
'The play was amazing'
Says one impressed fan.

Anthony Partington (11)
Our Lady of Lourdes RC Primary School

STORM AT SEA

As the water lashes against the boat,
The clouds storm across the sky.
The rain crashes along the sea top.

While I cry for help, the voice just echoes,
But the boat thrashes from side to side.
The clouds pass the moon
And cast a shadow among the water.

The storm calms down as I sail to shore,
But I'm on an island, which no one has seen.
I cry for help but no answer was found.

Paul Cooper (11)
Our Lady of Lourdes RC Primary School

MOON AND THE STARS

The stars sit there in their yellow shining coats
As they twinkle all night long showing us the way.

Then just as you walk away and turn the corner
Look up into the moon trying to sleep.

Then you walk out of the park gates walking home
Still thinking about the stars in their little dancing coats.

As you reach your garden taking one last look
At Mr Moon and twinkling stars dancing.

Cuddle up in bed still having good, sweet dreams
About your adventure in the park.

Snuggle up in bed without the dancing stars in their yellow coats
Sitting there all alone waiting for you.

There is Mr Moon wide awake
Mr Moon had a nap before the little dancing stars.

Carlie Sykes (11)
Our Lady of Lourdes RC Primary School

HAIKUS

The summer haiku:
>The seaside's quiet
>Sun glows brightly in the sky
>Wind glides gently through.

The winter haiku:
>Snow blows gently down
>The snowman stands so lonely
>Snow falls to the ground.

The autumn haiku:
>Leaves fall to the ground
>Crippling throughout the land
>Heard by everyone.

The spring haiku:
>The fresh air we breathe
>The singing birds we hear
>The sun shines brightly.

Christopher Simm (10)
Our Lady of Lourdes RC Primary School

THE FIRST CHILD ON THE MOON

Hi, first child on the moon.
How are you?
Cold, bored, lonely and frightened.
What can you see?
Trees, a burned down house and dead bodies.
What can you taste?
Blood.
What can you hear?
Nothing. It is complete silence.
Okay first child on the moon,
Time to come home.
'Hooray,' said first child on the moon.
10, 9, 8, 7, 6, 5, 4, 3, 2, 1 blast-off.
'Sir, there's a problem.'
'What?' said Sir.
'The fuel cell has gone.'

Lauren Garrity (8)
Queen Street Primary School

FIRST CHILD ON THE MOON

'Hi there first child on the moon.
How do you feel?'
'Lonely.'
'What do you smell?'
'A lot of fear.'
'What do you see?'
'Nothing but the stars and the Earth.'
'What are you going to do now?'
'Sit down and pray.'

Rebecca Amos (9)
Queen Street Primary School

THE THING

Creeping in the woods as quiet as a mouse
The ground is like a house
Longer and longer I walk
I can't stop to talk
There's nothing to see
But only me and me
I can't hear a thing
Except a thing go *ping*
Wait a minute, can you hear that?
Can you hear that *pat, pat?*
It's coming from the bushes
I look behind, it's . . .
     My mum!
You frightened me to death.

Sabina Ahmed (10)
Queen Street Primary School

NICE MICE

I like
Nice
Mice
Sugar and spice
Cats
Rats
I even like
Bats
Guys
Eyes
I even like pies
Mad Dad
I am so
       Sad.

Kirsty Openshaw (10)
Queen Street Primary School

I BUMPED MY HEAD

I was standing in the gloomy room
I watched TV - a funny cartoon
I watched Tom and Jerry
Then Kevin and Perry
I got dozy
I went to bed
I got up in the morning with a vase of roses
I was so shocked
I bumped my head.

Laura Holt (10)
Queen Street Primary School

SWEETCORN

Sweetcorn, sweetcorn is the best,
It's much better than all the rest.
The Jolly Green Giant makes it so sweet,
It's so tasty for you to eat.

You can have it for your dinner,
You can have it for your tea,
You can have it for your breakfast,
Unless you are silly, just like me.

So come on, get out there and buy it,
You don't know until you try it.
What delights it has in store,
You'll soon go out and buy some more.

Ben Flitcroft (10)
Queen Street Primary School

THE BATHROOM

The bathroom, the bathroom,
See how you glisten.
All these people talking,
You don't have to listen.

Your taps go *drip,*
And I'd give you a tip,
I cannot contest,
You are still the best.

Karl Pendlebury (11)
Queen Street Primary School

IMAGINARY GIRL

Creeping in through the house
Look over there!
There's something there
Cracking and clattering.
Look, there's something upstairs.
I go rustling and rattling.
Something's sweeping
Look over there!
Nobody together
Nobody bothers.
Look over there
The ceiling's apart.
Look over there
In a room there's a girl.
Arghhh . . .
Out of the door
Back to home.

Rehenara Begum (10)
Queen Street Primary School

CHOCOLATE, CHOCOLATE

Chocolate, chocolate,
Is bad for your teeth,
It's so sweet and sugary,
But it's nice to eat.

Chocolate, chocolate,
Stir it up in a pot,
Melt it nicely,
You'll like it a lot.

Danielle Smethurst (10)
Queen Street Primary School

SCHOOL BELL

Off I go to ring the bell
Rusty, old, unique
As it rings I hear it whisper
Ring me, ring me, ring me once again
Ring me, ring me, ring me once again.

Chelsea Smith (11)
Queen Street Primary School

CHEETAH

Cheetah, cheetah,
Go, go, go,
Sprinting through the jungle you must go,
High and low, you jump so fast,
To catch your prey on the dash,
And that tail that helps you dash,
Gives you balance while you dash.

Cheetah, cheetah,
Go, go, go,
Catch your prey,
Get your prey,
Climb up a tree and eat your prey,
Then when night falls munch away,
Cracking bones, a llama's nightmare.

Cheetah, cheetah,
Go, go, go,
Have your cubs,
And through the midnight with your cubs,
Teach them how to chase and kill,
And give them your lifelong skill.

Robert May (10)
Queen Street Primary School

SPACE

There's nothing
like space,
cold, cold, dark, dark.
No oxygen,
Just harmful gas, gas.
There are nine planets,
But more to explore, explore.
There could be more galaxies,
Well, who knows, who knows.
Space.

Abdul Wahid (11)
Queen Street Primary School

Fur Ban

F ur farming has been banned
U K's government stopped it not a minute too late
R SPCA think it's great.

F errets and other animals can no longer be farmed for fur
A fter yeas of campaigning, all fur farms are shut
R SPCA and other animal welfare organizations have got what they want - but
M any people are out of a job
I   llegal it now is and it's made someone happy - me!
N ow animals can live free
G reat! is all I can say about it.

Erin McIntyre (10)
Queen Street Primary School

SCHOOL DAYS

When it's time for school,
I leave at half-past eight.
I get to school by car,
To make sure I'm not late.

Our teacher records our presence,
By ticking through our names.
We do lots of things,
Including games.

My school is full of great things to do,
You'll enjoy your stay the whole day through,
So if you'd like to visit one day,
We'll be happy to help you all the way.

Lauren Baxendale (10)
Queen Street Primary School

WHEN I COUNTED UP TO SEVEN

I counted up to seven
then I looked up to heaven
and I saw a bird flying
they said I was lying.

Down came a plane
landed on the lane
people looked out
gave them a shout.

I sung a song
it was very long
I went home
washed myself with foam.

Danielle Keegan (9)
Queen Street Primary School

LIVERPOOL, LIVERPOOL

L   ots of fun every day
I   'm in Liverpool, hip, hip, hooray
V   ery tall buildings I can see
E   very building is taller than me
R   iding along, there goes a dock
P   ools are crashing on the rocks
O   h, it's good to be in Liverpool
O   h, it's brill and it's cool
L   iverpool, Liverpool, I want to stay forever
    but I've got to go home because we're having bad weather.

Hazel Hill (9)
Queen Street Primary School

THE CRAB

A crab is snippy,
A crab is slippy,
A crab is hard,
It looks like card,
It swims in water,
And it has a daughter,
And that's a crab.

Nathan Gammack (9)
Queen Street Primary School

SAND

Sand in your eyes
Sand in your bananas
Sand in your ears
Sand in your pyjamas.

Sand in your Vimto
Sand in your goggles
Sand in your pink toe
Sand in your ice cream.

Sand in your hair
Sand in your towel
And sand just about everywhere.

Craig Booth (9)
Queen Street Primary School

THE PARTY

I don't want to go there
I'll be sick on the floor.
I'll be sick like I was
When I went there before.
What if the jelly is too stiff to eat?
What if there's fat on wobbly meat?
They might give me bananas
All squashed and brown,
And custard to make sure
You swallow them down.
Please just tell them I'm ill
I'd rather stay here and be on my own.

Syed Uddin (9)
Queen Street Primary School

FRIDAY

It's 3.14 on Friday afternoon
The bell's about to go
A kid said so.
Pencils are flying,
The teacher is lying
The bell sounds
Let's go!

Stuart Parkinson (9)
Queen Street Primary School

AT THE BEACH

I want to go to the beach
but my car can't reach.
It goes too slow
so I just go with the flow.

Aidan Potter (9)
Queen Street Primary School

To Any Reader

As from the house your mother sees,
you playing round the garden trees.
So you may see, if you will look,
through the window of this book,
another child, far, far away,
and in another garden, play.
But do not think you can at all,
by knocking on the window, call
that child to hear you.
His intent is all on his play - business bent,
he does not hear, he will not look,
nor yet be lured out of his book.
For, long ago, the truth to say,
he has grown up and gone away
and it is but a child of air
that lingers in the garden there.

Rehana Khan (9)
Queen Street Primary School

SOLID

S and is a solid
O il is not.
L arge and small things
I t doesn't matter what.
D one for now, but remember one thing,
  if you try and walk through a solid
  it will sting!

Chelsea Scholes (9)
Queen Street Primary School

ODE TO THE POOR RUBBER

Once there was a miniature rubber
That lives in Lewis's pencil case but . . .
One day his life turned upside-down.
The pencil case started to crack,
Alas, a five-fingered object
Reached out and grabbed him,
So he got rubbed to bits.

Daniel Gammack (11)
Queen Street Primary School

NEW YEAR

Listen . . .
to the fireworks
crackling outside now
and the people shout
'Happy New Year to all.'

Jonathan Lang (10)
St Andrew's CE Primary School

A Witch's Broth

The ingredients in a witch's broth,
Is surely enough to make you cough.
There's eyes in there watching you,
Newts' tails, thick and blue.
Puppy dogs' noses,
As pink as roses.
Everything floating around,
Squeals and cries make a deafening sound.
They're all saying the magic words,
The stew's as thick as curd.   *Bang!*

Hannah Howarth (11)
St Andrew's CE Primary School

THE RAINFOREST

I see nothing but big, green leaves
and snakes blend in so well,
the soil is damp, the lake is clean
but what is that funny smell?

I smell the smell, it is decay,
the axe man's been around,
he's done his work, he's had his pay
but what is that funny sound?

I hear the sound of silence,
dear Lord this is too much,
we kill your trees and off we go
and leave no more than slutch.

I touch the mud beneath my feet
where once it was so green,
no trees, no plants, no anything,
oh, what a desolate scene.

I feel the air, it is so hot,
we've killed the ozone too,
it's time to stop and think again,
don't say you never knew!

So put your senses to good use,
do not throw them away,
or you'll regret, as will your kids,
come Armageddon Day.

Samuel Tomkinson (11)
St Andrew's CE Primary School

OUTSIDE

Look out,
Find what's outside,
The leaves are falling down,
The frost-crisped leaves break from the tree,
Then fall.

Mark Calland (10)
St Andrew's CE Primary School

BLUE BLANKET

A crustacean carrier,
A water barrier,
A fish feeder,
A seaweeder,
A wave wonder,
A rocky plunder,
A catalogue to make me
              an ocean.

Sophie Baker (11)
St Andrew's CE Primary School

Sooty

There was a lad called Sooty,
who ended up playing footy,
> when he won,
> he got his son,
to go and get him a butty.

Ian Wilkinson (10)
St Andrew's CE Primary School

POEMS

P oems are funny and sometimes sad,
O ne person might like it, another may not,
E verybody likes happy and cheerful poems,
M y family like poems, but not the sad ones,
S omebody may not, but at least it's nearly everybody.

Thomas Gidman (10)
St Andrew's CE Primary School

THERE WAS AN OLD MAN FROM SPAIN

There was an old man from Spain,
who wore sunglasses in the rain,
because he couldn't see,
he fell and hurt his knee,
and then got knocked down by a train.

Lauren Ainscough (11)
St Andrew's CE Primary School

SNOW

Look out
There is white snow
A big white sheet of snow
Shall we go and build a snowman?
Yes, let's.

Daniel Bailey (11)
St Andrew's CE Primary School

SNOW

Let's look,
A sheet of white,
There's snow on all the trees,
Let's play in it after breakfast.
Can't wait.

Matthew Storosh (11)
St Andrew's CE Primary School

JOURNEY TO THE END OF THE WORLD (VERY QUICKLY)

Joyce is doing twenty-four
Sarah and Carol fall to the floor
Joyce is doing thirty-two
Sarah's gone white, Carol's gone blue
Joyce is doing forty-three
Carol squashed with Sarah on her knee
Joyce is doing fifty-five
Sarah and Carol are barely alive
Joyce is doing sixty-seven
Oh is that them up in Heaven?
Joyce is doing eighty-two
Now the car is full of spew
Joyce is doing one hundred and four
Sarah and Carol fight for the door
Joyce is doing about two hundred now
All the crowds bow and say *wow!*

Nicki Russell (10)
St Andrew's CE Primary School

A LIMERICK

There was an old man of Catforth,
Who didn't bring his cat's mat forth,
The cat clawed his head
And claimed he was dead,
That poor old man from Catforth.

Benjamin Peter Healey (10)
St Andrew's CE Primary School

A WITCH'S BOOK OF SPELLS!

A frog's liver,
A bit of flowing river,

A pale dog's tail,
A bit of rain and hail,

A chicken's waddle,
A perfect model,

A catalogue to make me
A massive mouse.

Reham Jusub (10)
St Andrew's CE Primary School

KENNINGS

A human eater,
A wild creature.

A water reptile,
A spiky monster.

A pair of jaws,
A sharp claw.

A heavy tone,
A lazy one.

A dangerous log,
A colour of a frog.

A catalogue to make
Me a crocodile!

Suraiya Patel (10)
St Andrew's CE Primary School

A Road!

A car-calmer,
A place-taker,
A crash-maker,
A car-hell,
A catalogue to make me a road.

Kieran M J Peat (10)
St Andrew's CE Primary School

Dogs

D for dogs who we like so much
O for our dogs who we take on walks
G for gardens which dogs dig up
S for smell which our dogs do.

Jennifer Hails (11)
St Andrew's CE Primary School

JOURNEYS

Ships are gliding,
The sea is glistening,
Planes are shooting,
The air is soothing,
Spaceships are zooming,
Space is stalling,
. . . Journeys.

Andrew C Gregory (11)
St Andrew's CE Primary School

THE OCEAN

A shark-saver,
A ranting-raver,

A steel-ruster,
A sardine-cluster,

A coral-creator,
A whale-mater,
A catalogue to make me an ocean.

Christopher Jones (10)
St Andrew's CE Primary School

CINQUAIN

Look out
of the window
look it's snowing outside
There's snow all over the garden
Whooho!

Gareth Bennett (10)
St Andrew's CE Primary School

SUMMER

Look out
Of the window,
Sun burning in the sky,
Children playing in the water,
Summer.

John Parkinson-Jones (11)
St Andrew's CE Primary School

BILLY

There was an old man called Billy
Who lived in a place called Chile
He fell off a bridge,
Ended up in a fridge,
That silly old man called Billy.

Rebecca Claire Lee (11)
St Andrew's CE Primary School

CINQUAIN

Look out,
A white blanket,
Snowflakes fall gracefully,
Red breast robins hopping along,
Have fun!

Ashley Jayne Marie Pendlebury (11)
St Andrew's CE Primary School

A PERFECT POUNCER

A perfect pouncer,
A brilliant bouncer,

A furry friend,
A hand to lend,

A scraggy scratcher,
A wonderful catcher,

A catalogue to make me a cat.

Kelly Nicole Owen-Sing (11)
St Andrew's CE Primary School

AN OCEAN GARDEN

A green garden
A ship sinker
A coral creator
A cliff cracker
A wave maker
A tidal terror
A boat bringer
A crustacean crusher
A fish feeder
A catalogue to make an ocean.

James Penny (10)
St Andrew's CE Primary School

LOOKING FOR A . . .

I know a cat called Rocky
She is a black ginger mix
My cat has long whiskers
Her eyes are as big as a ball
My cat likes to slouch about on my black leather sofa
My cat likes to play with string
She runs round catching her string
On my fence outside she scratches her long nails
She likes to lick her fur
She always makes a loud sound when fireworks go off
And when I am not looking she pounces
For a juicy mouse.

Rebecca Howarth (8)
St John's RC Primary School

A VERY GOOD DOG

I see a dog
A very small dog,
Always merry and cheerful, never glum or moody.
He thinks I'm his playmate every day and night.
One bright sunny day the little puppy ran away!
Puffing and panting, then he stopped at a halt.
I picked him up, he hugged me.

I see a dog
A very large dog,
He's fierce, strong and a bulky dog, always wild with rage.
He started growling, jumping around,
He scared me and I ran away.
It started *chasing me!*

I see a dog,
A very cute dog,
Going to sleep in his basket, curled up in the warmth,
As it goes to sleep right now, it will rest as the day goes on.

I see a dog.

Ellen Lord (8)
St John's RC Primary School

MY CAT SAMMY

I can see my cat Sammy,
He has got long hair,
I can see him playing with
A teddy bear.

He likes to catch mice,
He plays with a dice.
That's my cat Sammy.

Lauren Walsh (8)
St John's RC Primary School

I SEE A COBRA

I see a cobra
All black and green
Slithering slowly through the summer sun
Gazing at a mouse
Its eyes are hard as diamonds
It's getting ready to strike
And *whoosh* it struck fast as lightning
Digesting the mouse whole
And now slithering away
Ssssing again and again.

Alessandro Re (9)
St John's RC Primary School

Dog Kenning

Play-ful
Nice- and cuddly
Long - tail
Wet - tongue
Loud - bark
Hot - breath
Fluffy - fur
Very - fast.

Richard Latham (9)
St John's RC Primary School

PUPPY DOG

I'm getting a little puppy dog,
I've waited for months and months,
We went to choose one yesterday,
There she was with her brother and sister,
All fluffy and white and cute,
Mine has a smooth coat,
Like a little white ball,
Tumbling, jumping and licking
Wow, wow, wow, I like the look of you
Please choose me, I want a home
Can I come home with you?
Yes you can!

James Walton (9)
St John's RC Primary School

A Dog Called Jessie

I see a dog, it is called Jessie.
Its best friend is called Bessie,
His cheeks are glowing like red
It has a very comfortable bed.
There is a bee who lives down the street
And the cows all do a beat,
I even saw a cat and a bat
Doing a dance in the street,
That is my dog called Jessie.

James Lea (8)
St John's RC Primary School

MY DOG MEG

I see a dog her name is Meg.
She is white and ginger
And very playful.
She always follows me
She is sweet, my dog Meg.

Jaime Burkhill (9)
St John's RC Primary School

BULLSEYE!

I see a rabbit called Bullseye
Light grey and fluffy all over
When awake just eats
She quietly sleeps
On her bed full of hay in her hutch.

I see a rabbit called Bullseye
She is such a good digger
When playing in her run
The troubles begin
With great big holes in the garden!
I see a rabbit called Bullseye.

David Summerton (9)
St John's RC Primary School

BRUNO

I see a dog called Bruno
I see a dog called Bruno
Bruno is lazing around,
Now he runs to me with his ball
I throw and he fetches
He barks at me in excitement
And I throw again
He is black and brown in splodges
His hair is as smooth as a pebble
He's smelt his dinner and gone in for it
I see a dog called Bruno.

Liam Short (8)
St John's RC Primary School

MY DOG

I have a black and white dog.
She's always up for a fight.
When she's tired she pants like mad.
My dog is furry underneath
And short haired on top.
She runs like the speed of light.
When she plays she never wants to stop.
My dog is called Tess.
She is a Springer Spaniel.
She loves my mum and dad.
After a run she's so mucky
She gets a bath.
All the muck comes off like mad.
She always needs a quarter of a bottle.
My dad has to wash her
And he complains and complains
And complains.

Steven Williams (8)
St John's RC Primary School

MY GLITTERY FISH!

I see a fish called Shady
She swims backwards and forwards
Exploring the tank all day
Shady a fancy fish
Pink, red and orange
Glittery, gleamy, shiny through the night
Shady swims silently
Splashing only when under stress
Shady my Chinese fish
I love her very much.

Chloe Vinden (8)
St John's RC Primary School

I HAVE A DOG

A doggie named Flossie
Licking her fur, you lick it quickly.
Your black and grey fur looks so long haired and fluffy.
You've stretched out, and you bark loudly.
You jump up and down while we're eating our tea.
Now you're going to your comfortable bed.
You're tired out today, you have had a long day.

Gabriella Dominici (8)
St John's RC Primary School

PUPPY IN THE PARK

I see a puppy, it is jumping in the park.
Spinning, jumping, leaping.
Black with white bits crouched to jump.
Sweating with joy, barking and yelping.
Running as fast as lightning he spins and spins
Right into the river I go to rescue him.

Deryn Rushworth (8)
St John's RC Primary School

I SEE A . . .

I see a hamster
Running round his wheel
He is moving so fast
he can't stop now
The shape is so round
His fur is so short
He tires himself out
And flops on the floor.

Lauren Greenhalgh (8)
St John's RC Primary School

I SEE A DOG CALLED TILLY

I see a dog called Tilly
Playing with her teddy
Tilly is running madly
She is as black as coal
Tilly has fur as soft and shiny as silk
She makes barking, yelping and panting noises
She likes to lick me a lot.

Sarah Rushton (8)
St John's RC Primary School

HORSE KENNING

I have a pet
He is very wet.
He is soft and very smooth
He enjoys his food.
You can stroke him if you like
But he might bite.
He likes to say neigh
His favourite food is hay.

Louise Jordan (9)
St John's RC Primary School

THE YELLOW COBRA

It's a dark and cold night,
You're in your bed all so safe,
You hear a crack, you can hear a *ssss,*
You get up, you look around
You see a yellow gleam, you go close,
You put your hand out with a shriek,
You see that it's a yellow cobra snake,
It hisses at you, it comes for another bite,
Your hand is stinging, you get a bag,
It slides away, you catch it,
You put it outside, you think it will come back,
It does!

Joe Lucas (9)
St John's RC Primary School

THE SLIPPERY SNAKE

I see a snake
It is slithering down the street
I see it out of my window
Going slowly
It's got black and green skin
It is in a slithery slope
I have touched it before,
It is hard,
I could hear it going *sssss.*
It poisons people if they harm it
I would keep my distance.

Jack James (8)
St John's RC Primary School

I SEE A DOG CALLED BABE

I see a dog called Babe
Barking and sitting down
running around in the back garden
She is grey, white and a shade of brown
Very small and thin
Her fur is soft, smooth and fluffy
Woof! Woof! She growls and cries
When she is on her own
Barks at her own reflection
I see a dog called Babe.

Olivia Dalton (9)
St John's RC Primary School

I SEE A DOG

I see a dog playing in the garden
It seems to be dancing around
Shall I go to look at it or
Shall I stay inside?
As soon as I look it always stares at me
And when I look away she starts to play again.
I think I'll go and look at her
And see if she notices me.
I'm at last outside I'm walking over to her
She stops playing and stares at me
I start to stroke her and she starts to lick me.

Lucy Corrigan (8)
St John's RC Primary School

SSSSNAKE

I see a snake
Ready to eat
Ready to pounce
Ready to leap
Coiled up round
There he goes
Eats the bird
And off he goes.

Alex Brown (9)
St John's RC Primary School

THERE'S CLEO

There's Cleo the brown and cream cat
Her fur's all smooth and soft
She lives next-door but one to me
She's Debbie's cat
She loves her bed and tuna
She's eight in human years but ninety-three in cat
She's very soft and gentle
She purrs and miaows as she falls asleep
In a land of dreams
What a wonderful place to be
Her bedroom is Debbie's
Purr, purr, purr miaow.

Rachel Pollitt (8)
St John's RC Primary School

I SEE A DOG

I see a dog
A very big dog
He is calmly sitting next to the fire
He hears a small purr of a cat.

I see a dog
A very big dog
He is outside licking himself
He can't hear me.

I see a dog
A very large dog
Calmly he goes to sleep.

Alexa Charleston (9)
St John's RC Primary School

MY DOG!

My dog Lucy is sniffing around
Looking on the ground
What has she found?
A bone? A ball?
Oh sorry, it's nothing at all.

Her fur is thick, short and very curly
Usually beige and white.
But at the moment she's very dirty
And now I will say good night!
I have to go and close my eyes
So I don't get a fright.

Joe Burton (8)
St John's RC Primary School

UNTITLED

One day these two seals
Called Ros and Mick
Were swimming in the deep blue sea
Silver balls falling from a storm
So the shark came called Rocky
Swam and knocked silver balls into a shell
There they stayed
Forever twinkling bright.

Ryan Jackson (8)
St Joseph's RC Primary School

UNDER THE SEA

Under the sea
Under the sea
Keep it a secret
Between you and me
Sharks and dolphins
Under the sea
Seaweed and crabs
Under the sea
Shells with a magic
Pearl in it
Under the sea
And it's magical
And peaceful
Under the sea
Lobster and starfish
Under the sea
And that's what
You can see
Under the sea.

Jade Rothwell (9)
St Joseph's RC Primary School

UNDER THE DEEP BLUE SEA

Under the sea I can see
A lifetime journey
Waiting for me

There could be
Some seaweed and treasure
Pearls and dolphins
Waiting for me
Under the deep deep blue sea

The fish go by
And say hello
And say goodbye
I go back home
Into my bed and I would dream
About my adventure in my waterbed.

Katie Worrall (9)
St Joseph's RC Primary School

ABOVE THE HIGH SKY

Above the high sky
I saw planets Saturn and Mars
And lots of stars
Astronauts in silver
Aliens in green
Up there you can see the scene
Jupiter, Pluto and Neptune
Go up there to see the moon
The stars shine brightly in the sky
You might see aliens fly by.

Sonia Girling (9)
St Joseph's RC Primary School

THE DOVER VOYAGE

I was on a voyage
On a ship,
Eating chips.
I heard a sound,
I looked around,
I saw a whale,
My face went pale.
It whacked the ship,
I hurt my hip.
Inside I flew,
My face went blue
And the whale followed me too.
We were near to Dover,
Then the ship tipped over
And that was the end
Of the Dover voyage.

Jason Cullen (9)
St Joseph's RC Primary School

UNDER THE SEA

In Majorca under the sea
Selling stones for 55p.
Mermaids swimming with their tails
Just beside her are a group of whales.
A shark is looking for something to eat
Something like a joint of meat.

Lauren Ratcliffe (9)
St Joseph's RC Primary School

A VOYAGE

I made a wooden boat,
I didn't know it would float,
I got some money and brought some honey
And sailed off into the sea.

I saw a great white shark
It was scrounging in the dark
Then I threw a little
At an unpleasant little carp
And sailed off in the sea

When I came back
My girlfriend gave me a smack,
My mum gave me a hug,
I plugged in the plug
And watched TV all day.

Callum Smith (9)
St Joseph's RC Primary School

A Voyage In The Water

I made a boat
I was hoping it could float
From shore to sea,
To infinity.

A big wave came upon the shore,
I was scared just before
I saw a whale
My face went pale.

I came to shore
From my big explore
I ran inside
From the tide.

My boat sailed away
For a week and a day.
It came back
With a fish on its back.

Charlotte Deegan (8)
St Joseph's RC Primary School

DEEP IN THE SKY

Up up so high
Where a silver shine goes by
Near the water far far away from me
Lives a shiny bumblebee.
Up, up in the sky lives a shiny star
In the sea, in the deep blue sea
Lives a blue shark
Up, up in the sky
I wonder how they fly
I know some have eyes
But I still wonder how they fly.

Craig White (9)
St Joseph's RC Primary School

MY VOYAGE

I'm going on voyage
In the deep blue sea
What if I see a whale
My face will go all pale
What if my voyage is under sea
And I see a shark I don't wish
But I hope I see a jellyfish
I want to have some fun
But what if I see a mermaid?
she might run
Then I'll go back on the ship
And sail back to land.

Rebecca Kearney (8)
St Joseph's RC Primary School

UNTITLED

T his is going to be exciting
H arry is going to be fighting
E ven though he's only young

V enus is the planet
O n a hot temperature
Y es they do love it
A round the planet are rings
G o to Mars to see the things
E ven though there's aliens there

I n space
N ow I better wash my face

S o aliens don't come near me
P eople go to space
A nd tie a knot in one lace
C ompleted this is the time to go home
E ven though we can't go to the Millennium dome.

Jason Harrison (8)
St Joseph's RC Primary School

SPACEMAN

I wish I was in space So I can fly
Up above into the stars and fly around
Then I would see the moon and my spaceship
Fly down and crash to the ground
Then I would walk looking away from the moon
Then I'll spin around in circles
And around and around.

Keith Raraty (8)
St Joseph's RC Primary School

SPACE INVADERS

S omewhere up there
P eople walk in the air
A liens live on Mars
C onquering the stars
E ven though you can't see them.

I think they are ugly
N ot as ugly as my Uncle Pugly
V enus is a planet really hot
A round the planet and in a gold pot
D ynamite might blow up Saturn
E ven if it does it won't really matter
R remember this for next time
S o you won't forget to rhyme.

Alyce Garrett (8)
St Joseph's RC Primary School

VOYAGES IN SPACE

I took a trip to space
I took an extra shoelace
I don't know why
Oh we're up so high
Are we going to die?

There is Saturn
Is it teaching Latin?
I'm taking a trip to the moon
I'll be a hero soon soon soon.

We're at the moon now
Is that that funny cow?
My story said it was on the moon
I'm going to be an extra hero soon.

Sally Fletcher (9)
St Joseph's RC Primary School

SEA

Under sea fish go by
Flying fish jump so high
Mermaids get on dolphins and race like horses
Seaweed gets all greasy
All horrid and weasy
And the octopus stretch
It's the spirit of freedom
Under the water.

George Smyth (8)
St Joseph's RC Primary School

UP IN SPACE

Up up in the sky
I wondered how the stars fly
And say go by
I wondered how you are quiet
I can't hear my light
I imagined I was aliens
Flying in space
And when I was in space
I saw a flying pie.

Michala Smith (9)
St Joseph's RC Primary School

TRUCKING

I dreamt of a tall truck terrorising
the tortured town that was as dark as the district.

I dreamt of a truck swooping through the soil
trashing trees, hoeing down houses
and crunching cars.

I dreamt of a truck driving through buildings
and beeping his horn in the middle of the morn.

I dreamt of going to sleep without a weep
and nothing left to keep.

John Knowles (10)
St Stephen's CE Primary School

VIOLENT VAMPIRE

I dreamt of an ugly violent vampire
With a face as mean as a vicious dog
I dreamt of a violent vampire with blood-stained furry fangs.
I dreamt of a violent vampire with claws as sharp as pointed glass.
I dreamt of going round the rear of the scary spooky forest.
I dreamt of a camera as black as the night following my moves.
I dreamt of the vampire catching us cold
And taking us to his personal party in his haunted house.

Daniel Barlow (10)
St Stephen's CE Primary School

THE VAMPIRE TEACHER

I dreamt of a teacher a vampire.
As slimy as snails, as sour as sewers and gasping garlic.
I heard pumping footsteps, as cold as ice.
I saw a white face, as white as a ghost
And as horrid as home.

Michael Pollitt (11)
St Stephen's CE Primary School

A Trip Across The Sea

I dreamt I was stepping into
An old smelly brown battered, school boat,
That smelt of rotten eggs
And looked like a peculiar pear.

I dreamt I could hear the rusty engine,
Clanking and creaking creepily.

I dreamt of the superstitious school boat
Crashing into a rocky ragged rock,
Which was as large as three extraordinary elephants.

I dreamt that ten cheeky children
Had to swim swiftly across the ballistic blue sea
Which tasted like a salty school of fish
And smelt as if one thousand sardine tubs
Had been secretly spilled into the wavy water.

I dreamt that when we finally reached
The interesting island where our scary school was
We discovered that one of the ten cheeky children
Had vividly vanished.

I dreamt that we were fine though
Because we freakily found her in the spooky school.
When we were in the school, wonderful Westlife
Were waiting for us.

Jessica Dempsey (10)
St Stephen's CE Primary School

CRAZY DREAMS

I dreamt of a frenzy of frightened dinosaurs
being chased by a terrific T-rex.

I dreamt of a room filled with
cunning cowboys and clever cowgirls.

I dreamt of a smell as strong as elephant waste,
a sight as vivid as the sun.

I dreamt my head was spinning as fast as
the great water rapids of Australia.

Lauren Cox (10)
St Stephen's CE Primary School

PANIC

I dreamt that I was on a luxury ship
I saw dolphins as big as London Tower.

I dreamt fish were in the wonderful water
and half of happy year six were with me.

I dreamt that I heard the whistling wind
and the water waves.

I dreamt that it ran out of peculiar petrol.

I dreamt that I heard seagulls screaming.

I dreamt of the sea as red as blood.

I dreamt I was hanging from the long luxury ship.

I dreamt the ship was sinking.

I dreamt I was in my bed.

Christina Bridge (10)
St Stephen's CE Primary School

EVERLASTING END!

I dreamt of having a battle,
In a gladiator arena
Where I saw rich royalty dressed in
Red robes as red as blood.

I dreamt of terrifying tigers
With teeth as sharp as razors.

I dreamt of hearing bouncing booing crowds
As loud as a crater crashing to Earth.

I dreamt of walking through
The great golden gates as I strolled along in.

I dreamt of staring statues glaring from the tower
They were glittering like gold with red ruby eyes.

I dreamt of the terrifying tigers
Being let out of their copper cages chasing me.
I knew it had to be the everlasting end.

Lindsey Arlington (11)
St Stephen's CE Primary School

MILES AN HOUR

I dreamt that I was a furiously fast robot.

I dreamt that my head was spinning at seventy miles an hour.

I dreamt that my back was a sharp as broken glass.

I dreamt that I had a flipping flipper.

I dreamt that I was as shiny as a dazzling diamond.

I dreamt that the disk sounded like one hundred humming birds.

I dreamt that I had an engine that sounded like a motorbike revving up to go a million miles an hour.

Zak Stuart (10)
St Stephen's CE Primary School

I DREAMT

I dreamt of a marvellous manor with
big doors as big as a polar bear.

I dreamt of a fabulous fountain with
water glittering like diamond and birds chirping happily.

I dreamt of a luxurious limousine
as long as a military submarine that smells of black car polish.

I dreamt of an absurd oak tree as tall as the Eiffel Tower
and leaves rustling in the calm wind.

I dreamt of a delightful dog that smells of a thousand washes
that is too scared to bark.

Timothy Berry (10)
St Stephen's CE Primary School

I'VE FOUND MY DESTINY

I can see the small blue waves,
Washing onto the shore,
They sweep the shore with shells.
Our blue boat has just landed,
I can see palm trees swaying in the breeze.
A small pond in the forest is filled with fish,
Dipping and swimming in the glittering water.

The sunlight dazzles my eyes,
It shimmers on water, turning to gold before my eyes.
A coconut, brown and furry,
I crack it open,
mmm, the sweet taste of exotic fruit.
And the sand, so soft, so warm, so comforting,
All I see for miles,
The shimmering ocean and the sweeping sand.

Caitlin Parr (10)
St Stephen's CE Primary School

VOYAGES

We will travel across the glittering water
With sharks and dolphins and fish.
We will swing from sail to sail, the water crashing
and flashing on the side of a boat,
Smelling the salty sea water.
The fog is getting closer and the fog gets thicker.
We can't see so we will have to go faster.
Suddenly, we see the sparkling island with gold and gems,
We paddle to the island very, very slowly and get the gold and gems.

Luke Haslam (10)
St Stephen's CE Primary School

I'M SO EXCITED

Buzz, buzz goes my drill,
I'm travelling by foot,
Pant, pant, this is hard work.

Yes! There's a gap, just enough for me to get through,
It's pitch dark, I'm scared!
Come on courage, I need you now.

Bang, clap and crack,
There's my lantern gone,
I'll have to do it in complete darkness.
There's a stalagmite and stalactite,
I'm boiling, I'm sweating;
What hard work!

At last, I'm there,
It's sweltering hot
But amazing.
I feel like jumping for joy.
Nothing could be more exciting than this,
For I am in the middle of the Earth!

Lydia Baldwin (9)
St Stephen's CE Primary School

A DANGEROUS JOURNEY

I'm going through the gold, glittering stars,
Maybe I'll go to Mars.
I am training to be a NASA cadet,
I've got loads of gadgets.
I'll be rich,
I will have my own football pitch.

My fear is getting stronger
And I am feeling weaker.
I see a strange thing,
It's circled with a ring.
It's Jupiter!

Oh no! I see an alien,
Let's get away quickly.
Now I see an asteroid,
This is what I was expecting,
I've got to destroy it
Or Earth will turn into a pit.

Bang! Bang! Shoot! Shoot!
Yes, I saved my most precious item
My home and the world!

Rochelle Richards (9)
St Stephen's CE Primary School

SPARKLING MOON

The alien went to the sparkling moon,
I wonder if he can hear that joyful tune?
The alien said, 'How I love that tune,
Why do I have to go so soon?'

Do you want to stay, my friend?
But it's really very near the end.
'Please, please, please, can I stay?
I promise you I'll sleep in the hay.'

We can't do that to you, my friend
I will give you space money so you can spend,
'Thanks a lot, thanks, oh thanks so much,'
And you can stay for some beautiful lunch.

Abigail Thomas (9)
St Stephen's CE Primary School

THE MOUNTAIN NAMED 'SNOWY'

The mountain is as big as a giant and is as white as a dove,
The mountain has never been conquered,
So let's go and conquer the mountain!
Up the mountain, snow is hanging off the cliff as if it
was a climber holding onto the ledge for dear life!

Click! Click! Click! Picks are digging deep inside the mountain
and pulling out lots of snow.
Halfway from the top, *Pant!* very cold, *Pant!*
Can't wait for a nice hot cup of tea, *Pant! Pant!*
Metres from the top! Oh no! what's that?
Aaargh! A bear!
Oh dear! Oh dear! Don't move!

The bear has gone! Thank goodness! yes! *Yes!*
Inches from the top
Pant! At the top, Yes! *Pant! Pant!*
Shaking with fright, *Pant!*
Stick the flag into the top. Yes!

I am the champion climber!
Pant! Pant! Pant!

Leah Shayler (8)
St Stephen's CE Primary School

MY JOURNEY IN A ROCKET

I wish I could fly
High in the sky
There would be a crowd
And it would be very loud

I'd have lots of fun
I'd see the sun
I'd land on Mars
And see all the stars

I'll see the moon
Which looks like a balloon
I'll sit in the rocket
With a mouse in my pocket.

Gabriella Hamer (9)
St Thomas Of Canterbury RC Primary School

A HOT AIR BALLOON

It is good to travel
In a hot air balloon
Soaring through the sky
I really think
You should give it a try
Well I did
And look at me now.

Michael Mealor (9)
St Thomas Of Canterbury RC Primary School

HOT AIR BALLOON

I'm in a hot air balloon
Soaring on high in the busy sky
Looking down at the ground.

I am so glad to be in the sky
Looking at the wonderful world
Watching the planes go by.

Christina Gordon (9)
St Thomas Of Canterbury RC Primary School

JUMBO JET VOYAGE

Flying up high in the wonderful sky
Watching the busy world go by
Flying up high in a jumbo jet
Asking the pilot to go as high as he can get

The blazing sun shines in my eyes
Higher and higher the plane will fly
Soon I will have to say goodbye
To the beautiful sky
And say hello to my holiday!

Sam Horrocks (10)
St Thomas Of Canterbury RC Primary School

I SAILED

I sailed, I sailed
To a faraway land
And there I saw lying in the sand
Some treasure, some treasure
There to be gathered by hand

I sailed, I sailed
Back to my home land
And there I saw with a look of fine pleasure
My wife, my son
Staring at my gleaming treasure.

Andrew McCrae (10)
St Thomas Of Canterbury RC Primary School

LEGEND POEM

Had I a choice,
I'd be flying with the harpies
Sailing with the argonauts
Adventuring with Jason.

Had I a choice,
I'd be seeking with Theseus
Duelling with a minotaur
Looking for Asiris.

If only I had a choice.

Etienne Littlefair (9)
St Thomas Of Canterbury RC Primary School

Magic Carpet

Bright night
Magic carpet flies

Bright night
Shining stars
Shine on the carpet

Bright night
Bats fly
Across our path

Bright night
Sailing through
The dark whispering night.

Amy Marlor (9)
St Thomas Of Canterbury RC Primary School

MY FLIGHT ON THE CARPET

One night when I lay
Awake in bed,
A sudden idea
Came to my head.

I ran to the spot
Where the carpet lay,
And wished my wish
Without delay.

I was zoomed away
To a magical land,
I felt like the world
Was in my hand.

And then it was time
For me to go,
And then I said
'Oh no, no no!'

Rebecca Connolly (9)
St Thomas Of Canterbury RC Primary School

A LEAF POEM

With a buffeting gale the leaf fell down,
Loop the loop all around, up and down, side to side
swirling and curling it glides through the air,
floating, gliding all the way to the ground,
there it lies on the green, green grass,
staying, not moving at all.

Thomas Tickle (9)
St Thomas Of Canterbury RC Primary School

MY TRAVEL TO SCHOOL

We were travelling along,
Singing that old car song,
When soon we got bored,
So we turned on the radio and Bolton scored.

It was a bumpy ride.
Well it was that or to glide,
When *bash!* my mum hit two bins,
But oops it was outside the twins.

I was wobbling and hobbling,
And soon was squabbling,
With my sister and brother,
'Stop fighting' said my mother.

Jennifer Hutton (9)
St Thomas Of Canterbury RC Primary School

CARS

Cars, cars, everywhere,
Zooming on the dirty black roads.

Standing ready to go to battle,
When the lights change green,
Colourful cars start to move, red, blue, yellow.

Cars going near and far,
Petrol fumes blowing round the air.

On the motorway,
Cars charging like troops in a long line.

I wish I could drive a car,
And some day I will.

Jonathan Montague (9)
St Thomas Of Canterbury RC Primary School

MAGIC CARPET

Magic carpet! Magic carpet!
Swirling and whirling in the sky
Flying over people who
Are pointing and staring
As I am soaring on high.

Naomi Cassidy (9)
St Thomas Of Canterbury RC Primary School

FALCON

The falcon watched the mouse like a hawk,
Right in the bright yellow sun,
His flaming red eyes spying on the prey,
With massive spread out wings.
Finally it's dropped, gliding down silently,
And grabbed the prey for its hatchlings.
Off it flew to the nest, watching for any danger,
Also for any more victims,
Passing planes scared the falcon,
On the long journey home.

Joseph Lomax (9)
St Thomas Of Canterbury RC Primary School

THE VERY BEST WAYS TO TRAVEL

There are many ways to travel,
And this is very nice,
If you could get some ice skates,
And skate around the ice.

There are many ways to travel
And it is really cool!
If you could swim around all day,
In a great big swimming pool.

There are many ways to travel,
But the best by far,
Is to sail on a pirate ship,
To distant lands afar.

Timothy Bailey (9)
St Thomas Of Canterbury RC Primary School

EAGLE

It has flaming red eyes
It glides through the sky
With a mean look in its eye
It stalks its victims
Grabbing its prey
Ready to strike another day.

Adam Smith (9)
St Thomas Of Canterbury RC Primary School

PLANE

Flying in the sky so very high
Zooming, speeding, gliding, soaring, tearing
Through the clouds with roaring boosters
Till it lands,
It hits the runway and
It is put in its hanger till another flight.

Dominic Crompton (9)
St Thomas Of Canterbury RC Primary School

ADVENTURE IN A . . .

I had an adventure in a submarine,
Down to the bottom of the deep blue sea.
Where all the fish could speak their own language.

I had an adventure in a hot air balloon,
I looked down on the beautiful landscape,
It felt like a bird flying high in the sky.

I had an adventure in a railway engine,
The fast cogs working away to speed it up,
The fields and hedges speeding by.

But the best adventure is when I'm in bed
In the land of dreams where I can do
Everything I want to, everything I want to do.

Amy Buck (9)
St Thomas Of Canterbury RC Primary School

HOT AIR BALLOON

In the sky it floats,
So high,
Burning hot,
Like a firing pot,
Floating up, up and up.

See the stars up in the sky,
When you're floating really high,
Floating down, down and down,
Onto the ground,
When the sun went down.

Nicole Walker (9)
St Thomas Of Canterbury RC Primary School

ROCKET MAN

Rocket man turning, twisting
Like a leopard
In disguise.

Round and round
Falling onto the ground
Round and round
There is not a sound.

Keith McNamee (9)
St Thomas Of Canterbury RC Primary School

BEACH TRIP

I put the pedal to the metal
As we zoomed down the road
Heading for the beach
We're here, we have a heavy load

Jumping in the sea
Playing in the sand
Might even bury your dad
Come on, time to go, give us a hand.

On our way home
Zooming past the farm
I wish I hadn't fell
And broken my *arm!*

Jack Gibbs (10)
St Thomas Of Canterbury RC Primary School

BIKE RIDE

As I climb onto my big blue bike
The world changes to a fast fun place
Where bushes and trees flash by like blobs
And when I end on my doorstep I will be sorry.

Amy McEntee (9)
St Thomas Of Canterbury RC Primary School

MAGIC CARPET

I wished the magic words
Without any delay.
I want to get out of here
Before it is too late.

I'm out into the sky
Away from that horrible place,
So peaceful and so quiet,
I could stay up here all day.

I will sleep on my rug,
In the countryside,
And go back home tomorrow.
So night, night.

Sheryl Court (9)
St Thomas Of Canterbury RC Primary School

LEARNING TO FLY

The bird jumped swiftly off the branch
Swooping and swirling
Twisting and turning
Down the bird fell
With a silent thud
On the ground.

David Hampson (9)
St Thomas Of Canterbury RC Primary School

UNDER THE SEA

I wish that I could go diving
In the sea
And meet some friendly mermaids
To show me round with glee
The dolphins will be nice
And take me through the deep
And that would be my wish
For under the sea.

Hattie Wujiw (9)
St Thomas Of Canterbury RC Primary School

SUMMER COMES

Summer comes with people bathing.
Summer comes with a gentle breeze blowing.
Summer comes with children swimming.
Summer comes with barbecues sparking.
Summer comes with little birds singing.
Summer comes with fish swishing.
Summer comes with flowers swaying.

Rachael Moffatt (9)
Westhoughton Parochial CE School

SUMMER COMES

Summer comes with gentle wind blowing.
Summer comes with children splashing.
Summer comes with children sweating.
Summer comes with treetops swaying.
Summer comes with grass mowing.
Summer comes with flowers growing.
Summer comes with treats for eating.
Summer comes with people cooling.

Ashleigh Brown (9)
Westhoughton Parochial CE School

SUMMER COMES

Summer comes with a gentle wind blowing.
Summer comes with treetops swaying.
Summer comes with ice cubes clashing.
Summer comes with children splashing.
Summer comes with people dozing.
Summer comes with people posing.
Summer comes with sea rocking.
Summer comes with grumpy hoping.
Summer comes with teachers nagging.
Summer comes with children bashing.

Summer comes
With . . . a good lie in!

Emma Wilson (9)
Westhoughton Parochial CE School

SUMMER COMES

Summer comes with birds singing,
Summer comes with wasps buzzing,
Summer comes with burgers sizzling,
Summer comes with heat burning,
Summer comes with flowers smelling,
Summer comes with grass swaying,
Summer comes with lazy days passing.

Tim Birkett (9)
Westhoughton Parochial CE School

A RECIPE FOR AN OLYMPIC ATHLETE

First sieve a great deal of talent in to a large mixing bowl
Then toss in a cupful of determination.
Now slowly pour in half a pint of technique,
Mix till smooth.
Add some evenly chopped balance
And a knob of training.
Grate some guidance finely
Then sprinkle this into the bowl.
Next incorporate courage with the spatula.
Start to add physique to thicken the mixture.
Slice support into large pieces, with health.
Drop this into the bowl with a dash of luck.
Combine the ingredients together carefully.
Let it rest so strength and stamina can develop.
Pop this into an already heated oven.
Whilst cooking perspiration will bubble to the surface.
After four years remove and turn out onto a warm podium.
Decorate with a medal.

Grace Roberts (11)
Westhoughton Parochial CE School

EPITAPH - FAMILIES

Here lies
Jolly old mum
Swallowed up by a monster
A monster so dumb.

Here lies
Golf-lover Dad
He choked on a golf ball
A golf ball he had

Here lies
Sister Madonna
She fell down a hole
And now she's a gonna.

Here lies
Brother so thick
It wasn't so funny,
To be honest, tragic.

Here lies
Doggy of greed
He swallowed a pip
More like a seed.

Here lies
A cat named Fuz
He fell off a wall
By the stop of a bus.

Victoria Catherall (11)
Westhoughton Parochial CE School

LIMERICK

I've got a teacher called Mrs Halliday,
She's unfortunately teaching me today,
I like her really,
Very dearly
Now I don't know what else to say.

Joanne Hardman (11)
Westhoughton Parochial CE School

REMEMBRANCE

Remembrance,
Remembrance,
Remember those who've died,
Died to save their country,
Died to save our future,
They gave us our future,
They gave us our life.

Remembrance,
Remembrance,
Remembrance poppies,
Blood-red poppies,
Grew where people fought,
Men fought in those fields,
They gave their lives to save ours.

Remembrance,
Remembrance,
Remember those who've died.

Fiona Hawthorne (11)
Westhoughton Parochial CE School

MENACING MAGNET

It draws things in then drops them down
Leaving the place not looking like a town,
Running around and about and up the street
Kicking things with its whirling feet.

Whistling and singing as it goes by
Leaving homes destroyed and making people cry,
Like a magnet attracting things up
Even people and a tiny pup.

Anne-Marie Booth (11)
Westhoughton Parochial CE School

TWISTER

We could hear the twister twirling by,
Laughing madly, whilst others cry.
It danced up and down a nearby hilltop,
'Stop!' we cried. It cried, 'I will not stop!'
It bashed the buildings, like a child!
But it was slowing down, going mild!
Finally it stopped, by the lake,
But then the stopping, had started an earthquake!

Rebecca Swift (10)
Westhoughton Parochial CE School

EARTHQUAKES!

Earthquake starting to shake:
Help, help, let's get out!
Don't sit there, or don't run about,
Take your children in your car,
And drive away not near; but far!

Earthquake; shaking:
The earthquake says, 'No time to pause.'
People think at how much trouble it will cause!
The earthquake collapses every car,
Nobody calls for help; no matter how near or far!

The end of the earthquake:
It's a disaster people will say,
They can't pay for the houses for them to stay
It's a murderer people will say,
It kills nearly everyone on that day!
It's amazing that it happens suddenly!

Mubarak Patel (11)
Wolfenden Primary School

FOOTBALL

Football
Is to share
A game
For everyone
Everywhere.

Football,
Should be fair,
Fulfilling
Man's dream.

Football
Should be true
To loyal
Fans like me,
Like you.

Safaraz Razi (11)
Wolfenden Primary School

WHO CAN IT BE?

Dear Mum

When you were out,
I thought I'll make a cake,
But somebody put flour everywhere
And they tried to juggle with the eggs
Unfortunately the eggs fell on our new carpet!
      Somehow!
The tap was turned on
And then there was a flood,
There were bits of jam everywhere,
Somebody was playing on your phone
Till the battery failed,
Who can it be?
It wasn't me Mum honest,
But you won't see me today
I've changed my mind
I've gone to Gran's.

Fatima Patel (10)
Wolfenden Primary School

AM I THE VICTIM?

It's happening again
I feel so frightened
What am I going to do?
The earthquake is here

The earthquake is shaking and trembling
Destroying people's lives
Making buildings collapse
Even killing people too.
What are you going to do?

Nicola Wilson (10)
Wolfenden Primary School

THE MATCH BALL

No one scored a goal with me
No one celebrated
No one wanted me
I feel a bit deflated.

Mohammed Hussain Bhaloda (11)
Wolfenden Primary School

EARTHQUAKE!

I shake when the plates say it's my turn
I kill loads of people but I don't really mean to.
People pray to their Gods.
They are petrified to go into their houses
Which are ruined after the earthquake.
It's a miracle how many people have been found
      after a week or two.
It's a shame houses are left abandoned and destroyed
I don't really want to ruin lives.
People all over the world come to help the victims
      of the earthquake.
Rats come along finding food.
The survivors of the earthquake get diseases!
I don't really mean to do all this!

Hussain Dhanji (10)
Wolfenden Primary School

EARTHQUAKES STRIKE

Earthquakes strike in Japan and India.
Houses, schools and flats fall from top to bottom.
People are buried under buildings.
Smells have caused rats to come.
Disease spreads, one to another.
Rescue workers help each other.
They come from different countries.
They work with community spirit.

Yasin Kara (10)
Wolfenden Primary School

DEAR MUM

Dear Mum

While you were out someone sneaked in,
Broke your window,
Smashed the TV,
Broke the plates and left them in pieces on the floor,
Burnt our new carpet with an iron
Let the dog in and there were muddy footprints on the
                                kitchen mat,
Left the tap on until there was a flood.
Honest Mum I never did it,
I have gone to gran's to see her.

Nafisha Patel (11)
Wolfenden Primary School

WHAT AM I?

I make the earth tremble,
I destroy houses like a bulldozer,
I kill people like a murderer
My children as tremors come after me but
They don't cause too much trouble,
There's nothing you can do to get rid of me!

It is a murderer, it's killing me and my children,
It has already killed my husband,
It's back for my children and our lives.
Please go away, I'll give you anything.
There in front of my house used to be a factory
But it isn't anything other than a meadow now.
A whole street of houses dashed into one another.

Saliha Sufi (11)
Wolfenden Primary School

DEAR MUM

Dear Mum

While your were out
Someone smashed your best mug,
The cat from next door jumped on your bed
And there were muddy footprints on the new carpet.
The window suddenly cracked,
Your best clothes were chewed
And the washing chopped into pieces.
Someone left the water running until there was a flood
And filled your shoes with sand and water!
Honest I didn't do a thing.
The new carpet was burned,
Your marriage certificate was ripped into pieces.
I didn't do anything, honest,
I've gone to meet Nan to help her with her chores.

Mubina Patel (11)
Wolfenden Primary School

DISASTER

I finally did it on Friday 26th January 2001
I had to, I didn't mean to, really,
I couldn't wait any longer
I wanted to show some signs of the consequences
        of him invading my territory.
It was his fault, not mine,
He victimised me and I responded by pushing him
He lashed at me and I lashed at him back.
The water pipes burst
Turning my territory into a swimming pool.
Please forgive me, I didn't mean to, really!

Nadia Matadar (11)
Wolfenden Primary School